Thoughts On Good Fruit

Fruits of The Spirit vs Desires of The Flesh

Arthur Lindsley III

/ BookLeaf
Publishing

India | USA | UK

Dedication

I dedicate this book of psalms to my parents, Art &
Connie Lindsley, who through their love and care set me
on the way that I should go so that I can even claim to be
living in this battle between the Spirit of God in me and
the desires of the flesh. Thanks for modeling this battle
well for me and being transparent about it so that I feel
free to share my journey as well.

Preface

Many have heard about the Fruits of The Spirit. If you grew up going to church they are a very common list that kids learn and a lot of the time in song format. They are Love, Joy, Peace, Patience, Kindness, Goodness, Faithfulness, Gentleness, and Self-Control. It's a pretty short list but the depth of the goodness of these attributes have inspired so many works of art, words, songs, and any who desire to follow God (or even just agree with a good moral system). The thing that children's ministry lacks, and I think rightly so (a kid's innocence is more important than telling them all the details) , is how to maintain these fruits while your flesh is telling you things in opposition of what the spirit says. These poems are meant to be a journey through the fruits of the Spirit and how I feel that the desires and instincts of the flesh have most commonly been in a battle against the Spirit in my life. I can't speak for you but maybe this will give you the tools to dive into expressing this battle for yourself or even recognizing it as a reality. These will be poems and by that form of writing may be a bit less direct and more big idea centered and with that it could be interpreted in many different ways. I want you as you read this, however, to come at this with an open mind so that you might potentially be changed by the descriptions of these fruits and the one who is willing and able to give them to you if you believe in Jesus, who made a way for us to God, and gives us, with God's Spirit the good fruits that He has to offer.

Acknowledgements

I thank the Lord for creativity and giving me the ability to do this work.
I thank the translators of the bible into english, of which, I primarily borrowed from the New International Version translation.
Thanks to all who have ever taught me and tested the way I think.
I am thankful to friends to converse with and wrestle through many of the thoughts I brought up in this collection.
I am thankful for family who has been good at handling conflict by facing it instead of hiding it away.
Thanks for reading this.
If you made it all the way through I hope it helped you think through a framework of how God gives us the fruits of His Spirit.

1. Love: As it is given by God

In the beginning there was Love.

This Love was, is and ever will be alive and available.
Out of love, God chose to create a vast array of goodness.
Light and dark,
Sky and sea,
Stars and planets,
land and vegetation,
Birds and beasts,
All of it was declared by their designer to be good.
Then God made a new thing.
He made something with the capability to love Him and
to be loved more deeply by Him.
Man and woman,
Made in His image,
Forged from dust and breath,
Never meant to experience death,
But there was a God-created condition
In giving human kind this ability to love

It was the choice.

Whether to love

or not to love.

Whether to listen to God's rules,

or to disobey and be separated from the giver of love.

This creation lay before them,

One untouched by the intent of mankind,

Filled with better smells,

sounds,

tastes,

things to touch,

And such beauty that we have never seen the like.

However, there was one rule.

You can eat of every tree in the garden

But you must not eat of the tree at the center,

If you do, you will surely die.

Unfortunately, evil had already entered the world and

taken the form of a snake.

This snake twisted God's good intent by saying,

"For God knows that when you that when you eat of the

fruit

Your eyes will be opened,

and you will be like God,

Knowing good and evil."

Because they saw the fruit was good for food,
pleasing to the eye,
and advantageous for gaining knowledge.
The man and woman chose the desires of their flesh over
the rules that Love had set.

Sin entered the world
And human kind learned about the evil
Along with the good.
Real love went into hiding
Until the day that had been decided by Love.
He had already developed a plan
To bring those with the capability to love,
back into a loving relationship with Him.

He chose a certain people and try as hard as they might
they could not work their way into love.
This only worked their way into judgement and the
endless sacrifices of bulls, sheep, and goats,
which were never fully going to cleanse that first sin.
A perfect sacrifice had to be made.
One with out blemish,
One that would fulfill all the law,
One that would turn prophetic words to truth,
One that would call all people to Himself,
But who could be so perfect but God Himself?
Who could fulfill all these things...

Jesus,

Jeshua,

The Messiah,

Son of God,

Born to a Virgin,

Never sinned,

Performed signs and wonders,

Preached repentance and the coming of God's kingdom.

Took on disciples and taught them,

Was persecuted by those he came to save,

Was crucified by Pontius Pilate,

Resurrected from the dead on the third day,

Sent the Holy Spirit to those who believe,

And while on earth His command was,

"Love each other as I have loved you.

And...

"Greater love has no one than this,

That he lay down his life for his friends."

The very essence of love died

So that those that He loved

Would be brought back into love

With their creator.

"This is love:

Not that we have loved God

But he loved us

By sending His son
As an atoning sacrifice for our sins.
Dear friends, since God so loved us
We also ought to love one another.
No one has ever seen God, but if we love one another,
God lives in us, and His love is made complete in us."

2. The Fruit of Love

We hear shouts in the streets saying "Love is free"
But someone had to pay for it.
We see the poor living life on the streets
But no one knows how to fix it.

Some say its the economy,
the governing, the somewhat broken way of things
But there's an answer of which we sing

Learning how to give when you get nothing back
Offering your services without pushing the salary cap
Victoriously fighting for those who cannot stand alone
Even if the cause seems hopeless you serve a greater
hope
It's love, love, for the sake of Love.

We've taken this love and twisted it to make us happy
And now we think we can buy it.
Industry and politics, democrats and republicans
Think they are fighting for it.

Love is not a one way street,
As if you could ever force your heart to beat
There has got to be a way to let you know

Life is springing up all around, 'cause that's how it's
made
Overcoming discrimination against those whom Jesus
saved
Voting ballots filled with ways to make this world a
better place
Enough of filling our pockets in this earth-based rat race
Just love, love, for the sake of Love.

Love may not fix everything right away
But it hopes endures and never fails.
Love promises that He will cast out fear
And provide you comfort as wind in your sails.
As you pass through those waters,
Love will be with you.
Through the wind and the waves,
Love has redeemed you.
Do not fear.
That is the fruit of Love.

3. The Joy of The Lord

Have you ever been to the doctor's office?
And they prescribe you with something to fix
Whatever is offset in your body
After they had run a few tests

Have you ever questioned them and said
"I know better than you" or
"I don't think you know what you're doing"
Then why would you go to them at all
And pay them your hard earned money?

Joy is like a good medicine given by God
to the people who need a cheerful heart
So when you think there is no one to help
Maybe try out a little joy for a start

Now that that is sorted out
Where do we find this Joy?
Is it hidden underneath some rock somewhere
or is it a secret gift in a box with a toy?

The good word says that God can pour it out
Like an oil onto your head that falls down your body
Or even like a river that makes His people glad

Joy, then, from its very source is from our Lord
Given to the glad in heart; perfected when we are sad
If we can find Joy in our mourning then we can find
the kind of life that Jesus Christ had

4. Joy & Happiness

I would like to try to prove a point
Solve a great debate that lingers on
It courses through veins, bones & joints
Joy & happiness are not the same song

Happiness is like a playful stream
In rain it flows, when dry it drains
or consider it a pleasant dream
Forgotten when you wake again

Joy, however, is much deeper still
It, instead, flows under the earth
Unaffected by drought or drill
Protected from where it finds it's birth

Many still confuse these two things
Either change or say they mean the same
Where the happy mourn the joyful sing
Compared to joy, happiness is tame

Now it's not bad to be happy and all
There is a reason for this emotion
When you see beauty or a baby crawl
Small graces but only a reflection

Don't you see what I'm trying to say?
Life is to be lived for the sake of eternity
There are some things that never fade
Joy will forever be emanating from our king

5. Peace: An Attempted Definition

Peace can be a dangerous phrase
to those who want to wage a war
Where we both put down our weapons
and see the monsters we've become
It's like the chirping of a bird
In a dry and deserted land
Bringing freshness to the ears
and water to the age-old sand

Peace can be found in the chaos
For those who have put off fear
Showing you can love your enemies
Will either heal or make them jeer
The flesh, it never wants to concede
Fighting seems way too easy
Swelling anger fueling hate
Feeling strong sealing fate

Peace is a choice all can make

But few have the strength to hold
For forgiveness comes from divine
And to set hurt aside is being bold
But we can't do it on our own
Peace, like water, falling from the throne
Stitching patches where none had sewn
For peace, we have much to be shown

6. Peace: Not In A Hurry

I'm in a hurry
To become what I said I'd be
If you know me
It's not what I'd thought I'd see

It's the struggle, the hard work, the only way
That I thought that this would come out okay

But He said, "Come to me"
What he did: Calm the sea
What I read in the morning
It comes into me
Peace
And not in a hurry

It's not always easy
To only get what I need
This is my one plea
That you will never leave
Cause I hurry though I know

It's doing me no good
If you're by my side you'll pace me
like you would

Cause He said, "Come to me"
What he did: Calm the sea
What I read in the morning
It comes into me
Peace
And not in a hurry

Rushing, combusting explosions of pride
Have never been what keep me alive
The faith, hope and love of Jesus
It's never a maybe or a just because
There's a reason
That we feel this tension
Through the joy
Forgetting to mention
The way - He paved it
The life - He is it
The truth is slow and steady

Cause He says, "Come to me"
What He does: Calm our seas
What I know in the morning
It comes into me

Peace
And not in a hurry
Hope
And not in a hurry
Love
And not in hurry
Cause Jesus
Is not
In a hurry

7. Patience: Taking It Back

This may be the most unnatural virtue
Who wants to wait for time to catch up to you
Certainly the one who waits, wastes
And the one who moves fast, faints
There has to be a balance
There has to be a cadence
This is called patience

It's not about lack of action
It's more a timing attraction
The one who waits is looking to strike
Like a lion in tall grass he hides
but only until the moment is perfect
Then he leaps like a banshee
And fills his belly and his pride

Patience has a scourned name today
We who know are taking it back
For in waiting on the Lord is strength
And in saving your energy for the right time

The right way is this, so...

Patience

Patience

Patience

8. Patience: A New Perspective...

Sometimes one wonders...
What would life be like as an insect...
Specifically a butterfly or moth or the like?

You come from your mother and then one version of you
is off and in the world...
Slimy, gross, slow, calculated, focused on the ground, a
bottom feeder of earth...
Sometimes one wonders...

You finally learn to use thousands of little legs as
efficiently as possible...
This brings you joy but then the earth quakes around
you and you can't run...
So you hide and perfectly blend into your surroundings...
But there are casualties in this game...
Large beings need to watch where they step!

Then you continue down the path to find a moving

substance...

It picks you up, turns you around, and flips you back out
on the other side...

This world is a dangerous place for something so slow
and small.

You begin to eat more and more of the ground you cover.
Grass, leafs, apples...

Your skin becomes too big for you and you shed it.

This happens until...

You feel an urge in your body to climb to the tallest
thing you see...

And without any one telling you, you create a hanging
home around you...

It feels like this is what you were always meant to do.

It so warm in there that your eyes start to drift off your
body curls in...

Time passes...life slows...but something is changing...

It kind of hurts but it also feels like a weight is lifted, or
at least shed...

The warmth starts to fade and you struggle to free
yourself...

After a few tries you see the first glimpse of light and
pull on the tear...

It opens enough for you to come out and you fall...

20

"Oh yea", you remember, "I climbed up this tall thing.
You spread out to accept your fall but only to find you
are gliding on the wind...
You have wings...Not only wings but colorful wings...
Where you once had slime and grime you now have light
and sight...
Where you once were slow and low you now are spry
and high...
No longer a caterpillar but a butterfly.

Now one wonders what some patience mixed with a bit
of providence creates
That's why the famous saying goes, good things come to
those who wait
The life we need has to go through a deeper change than
the insect
For trumpet will sound, and the dead will be raised and
none can change that.

9. Where Kindness Leads

Who, in these days, wants to be called kind?
The meaning has been diluted through time
What once was strong and true
Is now weak and misconstrued

If this is a fruit of the Spirit of God
And I know he doesn't deal lukewarm
Then this kindness is like a fire
This kindness's need is dire

As the world denies the very threads it is woven of
Turning what was once beautiful and innocent doves
Into piles of rubble and covered in the proverbial mud
So confident yet sure of nothing about finding love
We need a change...

A stroke of providence leads to a road
Better than a girl kissing a princely toad
For when we are humbled we can be raised
For there is none other to deserve all praise

God's kindness leads us to repentance
In the right frame we're ushered in the fence
The pasture for those who have eaten as pigs
God's arm, only, can reach into the pit we dig

So we have a creator who reaches to the fallen
He hasn't come for the heathy but the sickly
For he did not consider His equality by holdin'
But gave himself up, wore a crown that was prickly

He has shown where the path of kindness leads
Not to comfortability but to a life of sowing seeds
Sacrifice and suffering; faith over good deeds
The calling is following the one who holds the keys

10. Breaking Down Kindness

Kind has a couple meanings
Including what we bring
In our exchanges with
Other living beings
That's no myth

Kind can also stand for
Ordering any thing your
Senses can take in
And what's more
There's no end

No "ness" is and ending that
Implies the stuff inside, it's fat
The essence of the reality
Everything, good and bad
Fit in it's enormity

Sad, happy, large and small

Each have a "ness" to say it all
We have kind, good, great, strong
Qualities that make knees fall
To a God whose Love is long

Now let's bring it to this completion
"Kind" plus "ness" has explanation
All qualities of being good are now
Given to the broken ones and nations
Leading sinners to repentance
Providing paths past this hindrance
Accepting all the good, kind King allows

11. God IS Good

Jesus once answered a young ruler
Who was rich but we don't know why
And he called Jesus a "good teacher"
But none is good but God who never lies

This puts "good" into a better perspective
That most would simply choose to ignore
But if it's the most important thing to live
Then it's probably best to inspect some more

In the church today you hear,
"God is good"
"All the time"
"And all the time"
"God is good"
We then spring up with joy
And go about our days
What if we actually believed
That ONLY GOD IS GOOD

This means that God would send the good
Because we can't find it anywhere else
This puts the need on seeking like we should
Instead of looking for it in health and wealth

So say it with me,
"I believe that"
"Only God is good"
"Only God is good"
"I believe that"
He has the only right to declare
What is good and what to beware
So, in following him as our Lord and King
This will lead us to every good thing

12. For Goodness Sake

Just take some time to look around
Nature is slowly being used up by man
Many new developments and breaking ground
It feels like they are built on sinking sand

The news hasn't made it any better
Negative click bait seems to drive it all
They say if you don't know you're in fetters
Chained to the misinformed ones who fall

Instead of shaming others for steps we take
Let's change our ways for goodness sake

America seems hopelessly divided in two
No one seems to be able to close that gap
Instead of debating economy and stamping food
We seem to be crawling onto discord's lap

Instead we choose to hate those different from us
And be fully surrounded by those who agree

With every little thing we do in creating a fuss
Against people but we have a greater enemy

Instead of condemning for choices others make
Let us put on love and listen for goodness sake

Now I don't have an answer to these problems
But without conversing will it ever be found
Maybe we can't believe we can solve them
Or that "middle ground" is just hopeful sound

But what I do know is we need to not be fake
Real hope is true and do good for goodness sake

13. Faithfulness: As A Gift

How does the Spirit give us faithfulness?
Faith is something that God does not need
For in himself is all knowledge & holiness
There is no question of what will come to be

To stay on this point just a little more
God through His love sent His only son
Not to demolish sinners but save the sore
Showing that through Jesus, it will be done

Faith seems to be something God will prove
Both with miracles and with nights of soul
The blind will see and hearts will be soothed
From all we know faith fills the empty hole

God will always defend His glory and name
When they ask, "Will the real God please stand?"
He has sent down fire and forgiven all blame
Calling all people back to His capable hands

14. Blind Faith for Fools

We've all heard of the phrase "blind faith"
And we've heard "the blind leading the blind"
Now I think that wisdom sees these sayings
As a lot of fools and those closed in mind

Blind faith doesn't really exist at all
Unless one forces a poor decision to pass
For those who follow falsehood will fall
Like those who try to sail without a mast

Now certainly the blind can lead the blind
That's why we like sheep have gone astray
Though wandered off the path not left behind
For that would count as naught the price paid

This blindness is gone for the light has come
For the "blind" were only down in the dark
For the blackness is sent to where it came from
And with trumpet procession with the angels hark

Now when dying to yourself is what brings life
There is much more to see than we even thought
For light and life will ever give us our sight
And this "blind faith" for us will be forever forgot

15. Gentle As A Man

Male-hood has been morphed over the centuries
The messiah came as a man and showed many things
That many today would answer away or call naive
A "gentle man" could be the need in our becoming

Gentleness is attributed to small woodland beasts
Rabbits, chipmunks, mice, moles if you please
But birds of prey, lions, tigers and bears; oh my
And a mans mind favors predators in their sight

What are we to do if everyone believes it's lesser
To believe that gentleness isn't worth it's dresser
We are called to put on these things like clothes
Were we'll go when we do, only the few will know

17. More Calm, Laying Palms

More Calm
Laying Palms
At The hooves of
A donkey's coming
The rider presents as humble
All shouts no mumble
Glory to the king
They sing

Less mad
More glad
As men we strive
As paupers we die
We can't take one small thing
Up into the heavenly's
So live right now
Somehow

Gentleness

Not toughness
Is the way to sow peace
To see the golden streets
It seems we have it upside down
Who wears the real crown
Who we are to follow
A better tomorrow

Jesus Christ
The way to life
Never did he use his voice
He followed God's will & choice
So that, perfect, he might have all things
Subject, at His feet, to what He brings
Holy is the lamb who was slain
Bring us home again

18. Self-Control

Breaking down the words: Self-Control

Self:
A personal pespective
Of the souls directive
Pointing inward to an image
Placed there, a Godly visage
Deeper than we can dive
Knowing that you're alive

Con-:
With something or someone
Possible something to count on
Like confide, console, confuse
The with-ness you won't lose
It takes a context for anything
Even your soul's beckoning

-Trol:
Like alcohol, fentinol, erythritol

Addictive and poisonous to all
Mixing things together with science
Sometimes helpful, also defiant
Seems to raise inhibitions to rest
Too much could lead to death

With all these meanings and I hope we've learned
Control is desirous and causes fire to burn
But put toward a better truth and cause
You'll be following a new kind of law
For from the Spirit flows this ability
This self-control is a reward to see

19. The War for Control

This is where this whole challenge has been going
Declaring the war on your soul and what's happening
The flesh vs. the Spirit of God and who is winning
Though the Spirit does not force you to do anything

Sometimes it is good to just talk things like this out
Sometimes it is good to whisper and occasionally shout
For you have only a few true persistent enemies
That is your flesh, principalities, trusting only what eyes
see

They wage war on your mind, your heart, your soul and
strength
Which so happens to be, with which God wants you to
love His name
So make your decision because one last day will come to
pass
So in this life we should focus on the things that will last

Every battle in your life seems to get a little bit tougher

But every passing season the testing makes you stronger
The body will decay, possessions will fade, and one
remains
The one who has said that for faith he'll wipe clean all
your stains

20. Unfinished Song 1: In 50 Years

Who am I going to be
In 50 years?
Will all my shining qualities
Overshadow all my fears
Or will the sheer weight
Of responsibility and family
Turn all these hairs to grey
Leading body, heart, mind and soul
Slowly to the grave

What will the world be like
In 50 years?
Will science and progess lead us
Into peace with all our peers?
Or will greed and envy still be
The way that sinners have been
Wars and rumors of wars will rise
But we know how it will all end
We can't let our love grow cold

Before Jesus comes again

What will I be like
In 50 years
I'll walk instead of run
I'll update my way of fun
I'll say to all the younger folk
To live well while you can
And never take for granted
All the gifts you have
Given from God's hands.

What if I'm not around anymore
In 50 years?
What if heavens real and
I'll dwell with God forever
That is the place I'd rather be
But if I find that I'm still alive
I guess theres more work for me
Either way to live is Christ
And to die is gain

21. Unfinished Song 2: Yearly Check-In

Where am I
In debt
In nature
On an adventure
Learning new skills
In a new place
Not knowing many people
Not know exactly what to do
Doubting my abilities
Knowing my limitations
In the hands of God
Yet somewhat overwhelmed

Who am I
A man with promises over my life
Someone who dreams
But questions the quality of those
And usually ends up not chasing them
A Lover of newness of life

Finding new places, food, rivers, streams
Beauty, challenges, laughter, crying
Also a mover towards sameness
Once I have something I like
Unless I plan ahead
I go and do that thing I already knew
Or if I am in an adventurous attitude and don't mind
getting a bit of track
Some of the best things come
From those times of freedom
A lover of the Lord
A seeker of His truth
One who hopes for more in this life
As we will certainly receive in the next!

Who do I want to be?
A man who gives wise council
Not based on the wisdom of this world
A man who finds ways to flourish
in my own life
and for the sake of others
without compromising any morals.
Someone of whom it is said
"Loves others well"
Someone who receives love well as well
A man of more discipline than I currently have
A man of great self-control

And exceeding joy in all situations.
One who also is a deep-well
Offering those who are willing to dive
The wealth they will find in doing so

22. Unfinished Song 3: Modern Day Wisdom

Head up in the clouds now
Never thought too low
But I'm gonna fall down
Like rain that hits the earth
Only to join the rivers, oceans and streams
Then get picked by everyone else's dreams

Sit back in your seat now
And pull that buckle tight
It'll keep you safe somehow
Though we're moving faster than
The time where we smelled the flowers
Or when caught in torrential showers

Wisdom will come to
The one who sees it through
If you give up hoping
You've already started choking
On those bitter lies that you tell yourself

That you'll never see the sun
The battle can't be won
The race isn't worth the run

Wheels down on the ground now
Caught some turbulence
But you finally made this vow
That you'll live with better sense
Cause when the journey is over and done
You'll see that it's pain that grows you a ton

www.ingramcontent.com/pod-product-compliance
Lightning Source LLC
Chambersburg PA
CBHW070500050426
42449CB00012B/3055